Waking Wildflowers

Waking Wildflowers

poems of becoming

jess lynn

To all the wildflowers who wondered
if they would ever bloom

You will.

Table of Contents

Preface

WAKING

Every Story Begins   3
Let Me Grow   4
I Want to Be a Wildflower   5
Purple   7
The Longing   8
I Want a Life   9
I am No Longer Content   10
A Six Looks for Answers   11
To Be Gentle With Oneself (Part 1)   12
What is Good Enough?   13
Magic & Mayhem   14
Remember Who You Were   15
These I've Loved Since I was Little   16
Reflect Your Magic   17
Notes for Waking   18
It was Necessary for Me to Fall Apart   19
Wildflower Manifesto   20

DEATH

Sometimes Death Comes First   23
Absence   24
Scattered   25
Almost 40.   26
It Hurts   27
Bloodletting in Plain Sight   28
Worry   29
On Trying (or, what is still to be learned)   30
On the Rigorous, Uphill Climb   31
Ignoble Exhaustion   32
How could I trust?   34
Modern Self-flagellation   35
I'm the One People Speak About   36
Old Skin   37
Hard Hope   38
Even If the Magic Doesn't Come   39
Winter   40
A poem written while walking and listening   41
Unexpected   42

BIRTH

What is a Wildflower? 45
To Begin Again 46
Unhurried Welcoming 47
You Can Be Kind to Yourself 48
Insecurity 49
A thank You Note for Snowdrops 50
The Last Flower Crown 51
Hard Hope (reprise) 52
Remember to Delight 53
I Can Rest 55
Reminders for Being Alive 56
On Another Year's End 57
The Grandmothers Speak 59
A New Kind of To Do List 60
A Note to My Body 61
Today We Get Back Up Again 62
Reframe 63

RISING

I Have Not Failed Before I've Started 65
To Be Gentle With Oneself (Part 2) 66
Learn to Live Your Life 68
It's Not Time 69
I Hope You Will Be Gentle with Yourself 70
This Work 71
Words for the Pyre 72
From the Ashes 74
How Do I Trust Myself? 75
Pep Talk to Myself 76
Read Fairy Tales 77
A Request for Love 78
On Waking 79
A Benediction 80
Before 81

Acknowledgments 83
About the Author 86
Also By 87
Links 88

Preface

The poems and musing of Waking Wildflowers speak to what so many of us have experienced in the last few years—a dismantling and rebuilding of what and who we thought we were and a way forward into new freedom.

These poems were written between 2018 to 2023 and reflect the last five years of my life. Years that not only held the covid pandemic, but an unraveling of myself, past traumas, and much of my community.

While I've struggled with depression and anxiety since middle school, after the birth of my last child (and multiple miscarriages) I spent years living with generalized anxiety and regular panic attacks all the while still attempting to live my life as a mother, wife, writer, educator, and person of faith. When my faith community began to unravel in 2018 and continued over the next four years, I found myself alone and rejected while having to maintain an exterior of normalcy while much of what I believed to be true about myself and my world fell apart.

In 2020 as lockdown began, I realized it was time to step back from all my commitments. After nearly twenty years of keeping a nonstop pace with work and service alongside loss and transitions, it was then I met burnout. It felt like a train coming to a stop only to be hit with ricocheting cars that never slowed. I spiraled into a deep depression, at times wondering if I was sane. Barely able to take care of my day to day responsibilities, wondering how much more of my life would unravel as each day met a new turmoil in my faith community. Nothing was predictable or expected. Writing was my only safe space.

The poems in Waking Wildflowers are a reflection of these seasons. In **Waking**, the poems chronicle the desire and yearning for something more, as well as frustration and fear that there's nothing more. It's the dissonance of hope mixed with fear and anger at the betrayal we've done ourselves, but still there is a child's confidence that just maybe there is more to be imagined if we're willing to open the door. In **Death**, the poems explore the stripping of the old self and the discomfort in learning the way of gentleness, as well as all the ways we've tried and failed in the past, trusting oneself to the process that things must die in order to be reborn.

In **Birth**, the poems center around a new way to live and telling yourself a different story of what is possible, but also how growth isn't linear. You're not done yet, seeds are rising. In **Rising**, the poems share in the work of healing. Even then, there is not an end date to healing and rising, but a continual becoming.

I hope *Waking Wildflowers* gives you breathing room. I hope you'll glimpse a reflection of yourself in these scribblings. I hope it tastes like courage and smells like damp earth after rain. I hope it feels like expansion and sounds like an invitation.

I hope you feel the call to wake up.

Jess Lynn

Content Warnings: depression, anxiety, self-harm, miscarriage, emotional abuse

Waking

Every Story Begins

Every story begins with a door.
Splintered wood with peeling paint,
Impenetrable solid stone, or a paned window
casting blurry vision.

There is a door within all of us.

You must knock or turn the knob.
The choice is yours, to stand
and wonder what is on the other side.
To question the cost, hand shaking—reaching.

But every story begins with a door
and before it begins, you must open it.
And—if you're brave enough,
to walk through.

This is a door to awakening,
but before opening is wonder, trepidation.
Walk through and you may find
yourself waking up.

Let Me Grow

let me grow as a vine
reaching toward the sun

weaving through broken places
blooming in shadows

crawling, climbing
finding my way

seeking patches of light
that I may find

who I am

I Want to Be a Wildflower

I want to be a wildflower
breaking through the ground
Pushing through the darkness
reaching for the sun

I want to be a wildflower
grateful for winter's rest,
Death hiding in dirt
Rebirth hiding in death

I want to be a wildflower
who respects the cold, hard ground
And knows the weight of wonder
wrought within her roots

I want to be a wildflower
who--when she hears the sun,
does not doubt it calls to her
And breaks through the soil

I want to be a wildflower
who's not afraid to try
and knows within herself
wonder and magic reside

I want to be a wildflower
pliable, yet strong
who knows she is worth
unapologetic blooming

I want to be a wildflower

Purple

I sat beside friends
as the teacher read my words
words I didn't know would be read aloud
words of purple beauty freedom
they lauded my use of
alliteration, consonance, simile
leaned over and listed them
as the teacher read
smiling, proud of me
and I sat shocked
still
someone valued my words
those I wrote from my heart
spilling forth fields of flowers
from a fictional Italian countryside
wrapped in Lucy's heart
I stood to be inducted into
the national honor society
in my black pants and
gray button up shirt
hair slicked back into a pony,
that little rebellion riotous with curls
monochromatic at seventeen
nothing like the purple wildflowers
of my heart
locked away in tepid gray
If purple breathed in color
it'd be a room with a view
and a girl clambering
to open the windows

The Longing

What do I do?
How will I rest?
The question I am asking:
What will make me happy?

I want a life that isn't pretending or always waiting or preparing. I want to enjoy my life, not be exhausted by it.

I am no longer content with just being quiet.   *Am I?*
I'm carrying the dissonance in my body.
And it hurts.

A Six Looks for Answers

I live like the secret of life is
being over prepared,
so I am always prepping
catastrophizing
my life is lived in lists
  color-coded
  itemized
yet still, still
I am not prepared,
never ready
to live.

What answers do the poets have?
(even this is written in pencil. it can be erased.
a mistake. an error. a shame to hide.)

To Be Gentle with Oneself (Part 1)

I do not know how to be gentle with myself
I was not taught gentleness
I was taught
  hard work
  striving
  prove them wrong
  don't show weakness
To be gentle was to let the cracks show
To admit that maybe you didn't have what it takes
      (but you could never show that
      never let the enemy know)
Perhaps,
that's what I fear
Perhaps,
that's why I can't let go of my lists and hard exterior
Perhaps,
I am afraid
I don't have what it takes
to be gentle

(but, oh, how I want to be)

What is "good enough"?

the chasm creaks
hunger in its bowels
eager to devour
never satisfied

suffocating under its weight
I prod the beast
desperate to know

—this, this
I must hinge my worth upon

Magic & Mayhem

There is magic and mayhem in all of us,
we just need to know which way to
channel it on any given day.

Remember

Remember who you were
before they littered you
with lies.

These I've loved since I was little

Dandelion heads, the smell of paper,
Walking the aisles of bookstores,
old ladies singing "Hallelujah!,"
grass under bare feet, a breeze on
summer's sweat
Tea that's grown cold, fireflies at dusk,
old houses, flowers on the side of the road,
a pretty dress to twirl in, a good classic romcom,
lines of a family tree
A stack of books so high I won't read them all,
Mawmaw's pound cake, my favorite pens,
A new bottle of nail polish, laying on the grass
Watching ants, birdsong in the morning, happenstance
of afternoon naps, a nest of pillows

Rebirth looks a lot like childhood.

Reflect Your Magic

Let your life reflect your magic, not your fear.

I will be open and listen for the sound of the deeper well, the deeper waters.

Notes for Waking

You don't need to apologize for your presence.
In fact, don't.

You are worth more than your productivity. End of story.

Don't believe the lies that you only matter based on how much you give of yourself. Even if it's reinforced by people leaving you when you slow or stop your productivity.

The payoff for staying stuck is to hold myself back from being the wildflower wonder I see myself as.

Not everyone will agree with you. This is normal.

Not everyone will stand beside you and love you anyway. This will hurt.

You will be surprised by those who stayed.

Only you can live your life, stop parading for the visible and invisible "them."

It was necessary for me to fall apart

It was necessary for me to fall apart.
This breaking is a gift in disguise
though there were days I'd rather
I never opened it
Preferring the safe and familiar,
though it taxed me,
broke my soul and left me dry
eroding the hope I held into tatters,
still the known was preferable
to what might be on the other side

What if I broke
only to be captured again?
Torn up worse than before

But it was necessary for me to fall apart.
To feel the shards in each painful step
telling me I was alive
The constant prick and bleeding
a telling, a doorway and reminder
that coming or going or staying
there would still be shards

The falling apart became an unwelcome grace,
A silent rebellion to not give up,
not be content, to will a door to open
to another way and walk through

Wildflower Manifesto

One day we will be
fully awake, fully alive
We'll stretch our leaves to the dawn
and bloom as we were born to all along

for now,
we are waking
don't despise our small beginnings
the tiniest seed

for one day
we will be a field of gold,
of crimson and clover,
of blossoms painting fields
That will bring you to your knees

The birds and bees will flock to us,
their sweet sustenance, and we will
ravish the world with the
beauty of our wonder

be ready,
one day you'll look and see
the world abloom with wildflowers
who were too much to tame

Death

Sometimes Death Comes First

before we bloom
we must fall
a seed to the earth
death comes for us all
and yet so does rebirth

Absence

I have learned not to feel,
(I have taught myself not to feel)
   I tell myself.

It is easier to be numb,
(to close myself off from the world)
   to feel nothing.

But in feeling nothing,
(There is nothing I can control)
   I feel the absence
   of everything
(to feel everything)
and then I cry.

I feel scattered, like I'm trying to gather the pieces of myself and I can't. So, I just huddle in a ball on the ground and watch as the pieces swirl around. I am disembodied and fractured and not in enough control to pull myself together. How do I pull myself together without being a detriment to myself?

-make a list, then organize it by priority

Almost 40.

You told yourself
by 25 you should have this all figured out
Who you were going to be
What you were going to do
The vision you had,
The freedom you craved.
You tasted it, at 25.
But, so young.
You thought that life would be
easier, fuller
if you know who you were.
You didn't yet know that
the only way to know yourself
is to keep on living
and changing.
A river carving the banks
year after year, in flood and drought
25 is so early to know yourself fully.
Even at 40, we've yet to know
all the versions of ourselves
we will become.

It hurts

it hurts
out growing
your old skin

no one
expects the snake
to never shed

even dust
gathered in corners
are organic remains

it is normal
to grow and
change

we can never be
all that we once
were

and still
become
who we will

Bloodletting in Plain Sight

Hide your pain where they can't see
Cover up your scars
Don't let the blood drip
You can't let them know
the multitudes you hold

Why is it that worry feels like it's doing something?

On Trying (or, what is still to be learned)

I'm not so much afraid of trying as I am afraid of trying on the wrong thing and finding it a waste.

**on the rigorous, uphill climb of learning to be gentle
with oneself**

I am annoyed
tired
try harder
I have
it doesn't work
why can't you?

ignoble exhaustion

I said I'd be gentle with myself
this year, this summer
It makes sense, kindness
   to one's self
   your soul, your mind, your body
It craves it, flourishes under
   kind and gentle intention,
   practice.
I wouldn't know.
My mind and body are
   out of sync
My body says, *Please rest,*
   be gentle with us. The work
   can wait.
My mind screams back, "No!"
   caffeine in hand, red-rimmed eyes,
   "We have to get this done!
   There's not enough time.
   We're so far behind.
   There's not enough time."

There's not enough me.

And I don't know how to tell my mind
that it's okay to breathe
that every fear won't be realized.

But I don't know, what if they will?
And then, my mind will have been right all along.
But what then?

How will my body fare?
Half-gone? Spent in ignoble exhaustion?
crawling toward success, bones brittle
heart barely intact
striving, striving, striving
for something I wonder if gentleness can give

How could I trust—
a year later

I searched,
afraid of what the answer would be.
How could I know—
How could I trust—
that gentleness was the way?

Modern Self-flagellation

But if I don't punish my body, how will I know I worked hard enough?

I'm the one people speak about in concealed whispers. Wondering if she's okay because she's not quite like who she once was.

I don't always know how to be okay with that. The whispers and being not who I once was.

Old Skin

I am shedding old skin / This casing was never meant to stay / New wine in old wineskins I will burst / Splatter, pour forth, and then it won't be a pretty blossoming, but an arcane, savage splatter / without room to breathe, finger circling the ring of the glass, I will combust / bury me deep, paper thin garments laid in the earth, cover me / dark earth dancing in it / lay me in my tomb. let me rest / I am shedding old skin

Hard Hope

I don't mind the dark so much anymore. I prefer wandering to pithy responses and pats on the back, as uncomfortable and lonely the dark may be. I'd rather hold an honest candle with you in the dark, than pretend all is well and right.

I stand in the shadowlands with this faltering, fragile flame—this hope, exposing the cracks in my soul and in systems and places I once trusted. The light must get in somehow.

I still stand, holding tiny embers. These flames may pale in comparison to what we wish is or what was or the unknown of what will be, but even when it's hard to hope—when everything feels untrue, still I hold my meager offerings in the dark.

Hard hope,
struggling hope,
dim hope
is still hope.

Even if the magic doesn't come.

Even if the magic doesn't come.
Even if the growth can't be seen.
Dig anyway.

Winter

Winter exposes our branches
We can no longer hide in the shade of green
Laid bare, amidst gnarled
roots and fungi limbs

The wind blows bitter
and we shiver
no longer surrounded by
summer's raiment

Winter has a way of revealing
our brokenness. Of exposing
the places that need pruning,
places we've hidden

The fractured splintering of
this roughened skin endures
until Spring buds anew and
we grow our own vestments

A poem written while walking and listening

Spring hangs in layers
The birds come first
Their cries at tree height
Then the wind, wrestling
east to west, vacillating
            between cold and warm fronts
Unable to make up its mind.
Last are the flowers,
tentative—
knowing if they reach too soon
death may come for them—
be it frost or flood.

I am the birds…
            ever hopeful

I am the wind…
            uncertain of where I should go

I am the plants…
            risking death to live.

Unexpected

the way tears spill
unbidden
at the sight of
tiny wonders
or stars scattered

the catch of breath
to find a scrap
reminder of
a time before
broken yet whole

reminiscing
to weary souls
that what has died
still lives in memory
waiting to be reborn

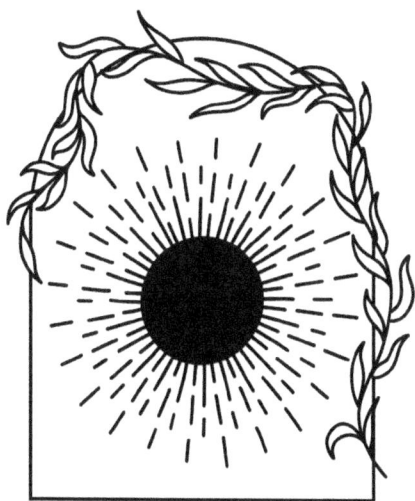

Birth

What is a wildflower?

A wildflower is pliable, not manipulated, blows in the breeze, but sturdy. Wildflowers blossom in various climates and habitats, and are adaptable; they grow free without intervention.

A wildflower belongs to itself.

"It sounds like you don't believe you deserve to be here."

Oh, but I don't believe it. But I'm going to do it. Show up anyway. Because that's what wildflowers do.

We grow where we're least expected, between stones and on brick walls, along roadsides filled with exhaust and in meadows not our native home, carried in excrement of flying friends.

Wildflower, grow wherever you are.
Belong to yourself.

I am and I will.

To Begin Again

To begin again
hurts
to know it wasn't
enough the first time

is to assume
beginning is perfection
sifted, weighed, and
wanting

with clarity to see
what was blind before
hidden in crevices
doubts lurk

unaware
to begin again
is to assume
a kindling of sorts

Unhurried Welcoming

spinning on Earth's axis
for such a time as this
each season is its own

You Can Be Kind to Yourself

You can be kind to yourself.
You can be kind to yourself.
You can be kind to yourself.
You can be kind to yourself.
You can be kind to yourself.

Insecurity

Insecurity, I offer you compassion for helping to protect me.
Insecurity, I offer you compassion for being a defense.
Insecurity, I offer you compassion.

a thank you note for snowdrops

snowdrops,
thank you—
for blooming
in the harshest conditions
through frozen dirt and rain
frost settled on your petals
you are not a white flag of surrender
but the ringing bell's of survival

my dear,
we all are made for different seasons
the cold is mine.

sincerely,
snowdrops

The Last Flower Crown

Sometimes it's hard to hope. To look at what is and what was and what may be and see anything other than darkness and failure, flaws and pain, toil and trauma, and find yourself anywhere other than the ecclesiastical loop of "everything is meaningless."

It's hard to stand in the dark and believe the Light, when doubt, fear, and self-loathing flood. When cries of "How long?" and "Why?" are met with the silence of the stars. When the old words of "wait and hope," that ancient comfort, are dragged out and run dry. When you know what you're supposed to say, what you're expected to say, but can't bring yourself to say. Sometimes it's hard to hope.

Hard Hope (reprise)

I don't mind the dark so much anymore.
It's there, in the far reaches
of the night that
light still breaks through.

I have not been left,
you have not been left.
Hold out your light.

Remember to Delight

Remember to delight.
Remember how to delight,
It's tucked deep inside.

And if you cannot, if
delight feels foreign on your lips,
a remembrance of a time
When you were young and free,
before the clouding pain and doubt
Gently knock on the exile's door
and beckon it to come remind you.

If delight is hidden behind a door,
locked behind windows,
safe from naysayers and prying eyes,
Seeing and wishing but
Never feeling the joy of a
breeze on your face,
Or how the petals graze your fingertips

Be gentle.
Bring it a gift,
a token of affection and appreciation.

Invite it to join you in fields of gold
as you frolick, lay in the grass,
meander through the years
awakening dormant places within
opening the eyes of heart and mind
cultivating a safe space to

test the waters of delight.

And, when you dip your toe
in the bubbling brook
may you remember all that brings
you joy. May the gurgling, cold
shock you into joy's remembrance.

And, dear one, may it stir in you
hidden delight, beckoning to overflow
and may you smile uninhibited and learn
to love yourself again, as you
remember to delight
in this life with all
its magic and mayhem

I Can Rest

I can rest without fear of losing my creative momentum.
I can rest without fear of losing my creativity.
I can rest without fear of losing.
I can rest without fear.
I can rest.

Reminders for Being Alive

You are not defunct or lacking or worthless.

You are good and imaginative and whole.

You are allowed to nurture yourself.

There is no shame in realizing all you did not know.

On Another Year's End

When you start to feel like
things should have been better this year,
Look back and see the truth—

The years are quick, but the days long and
I forget the good in the haze of life's work.

In my exhaustion, weariness, anxiety, and brokenness
I see all my fears played out, my failings,
all the ways I lacked.

I wear the heaviness of hard conversations
and forget the healing in them.
I heave loneliness in the dark and neglect
all the smiles, laughter, and necks hugged.
The voices that said it's okay to cry,
The ones who took my crazy and prayed
with me anyway, those who held me when
my body racked and the ones who laughed
with me at the days to come in song and
GIF and text and words.

I see all I've left undone and I forget the
new paths tread.

I see darkness and chaos and I forget
the rays of light, the feel of a
butterfly's wing, the wonder and worship
in a crown of flowers.

I see the mother I was not and mourn,
turning the tongue's knife inward,
but I forget the hugs of "I love you mommy"
and the middle of the night cuddles and
the resilience of children and their love.

I feel the weight of all I am not
knocking the scale off balance.

I am the dreamer drowned, but
I look back up under the waves and
see a million tiny bubbles of air
rushing to burst into life.

I see flowers and laughter and imagination
and joy. I see weariness and work. I see
longing and straining. I see hope.

The Grandmothers Speak

Hold your head up, baby
Don't let them see you cry
They don't got to understand
You be who you are
You come from something,
    you know that, right?
Baby girl, hold your head up high
They can't take nothing from you
    that you ain't given them first.
So don't let 'em
You've got this
Keep walking
Keep your head up
The Grandmothers are watching
How you think we lasted this long?
Baby girl, be strong.
Not for them, no they don't need
    your strength
Be strong for you—
    with a spine straight as a pine.

A new kind of to do list:

What do I want?
How can I become more of myself?
How can I heal this year?
What are areas that need tending?
What do I need today?

A note to my body

I don't want to hate you. I'm sorry I do. I've felt let down and
disappointed.

Death and life have mixed in my womb
and I am a woman who's failed the litmus test to nurture

My body dispeled, aborted
what I was desperate to hold

I am a walking contradiction
lacking control of my primeval instincts

I have been shamed and shamed you in return
flailed and raged
stuffed and starved
Beat and despised

And yet, still this body
pumps blood through my veins
held my grief and broken bones
and let me rise

This is a new way, isn't it?
To not hate all the places we've been
all the places you've carried me

Today we get back up again. Today we take the kindled dreams and stoke the fire.

Reframe

Look for possibility, not past failures.
Look for possibility, not anticipate struggles
Look for possibility, not unspent devastation.
reframe, reframe, reframe

Rising

I have not failed before I've started.

To be Gentle With Oneself (Part 2)

To be gentle with oneself
   is a work of art.

To hold oneself,
   tender and reverent
   to the light just to admire
   the corona.

To be gentle with oneself
   as a work of art
is to know your worth
        your singularity
        your value

I am still learning to be gentle
   with myself
(it's easier to see the art in others)
I often throw myself around
like dirty kitchen towels and stinky shoes
whirling and knocking in the washer
hoping, that at least the job
   gets done.
Even if the wash is a little rough
I'll be useful.

~~I do not see myself as a~~
~~work of art.~~
I am learning to see myself
as a work of art.
To hold myself, gently

to the light
and not first think of the
cracks and frays,
but to grasp softly
the tender places
and look with grace
upon my crown.

Learn to love your life with all its disruptions, this too is a gift. Healing didn't derail you. Burnout didn't derail you. Falling apart didn't derail you. This too is a gift.

It's Not Time

You can do this.
You are doing this.
It's not time to give up.
Not yet.

I hope you will be gentle with yourself.

I hope you will be gentle with yourself. I hope you will allow yourself gentleness. To breathe and know the next step doesn't need to be figured out. I hope you are able to stand, lay, sit, float, laugh and know you are okay. I hope you know gentleness is always a possibility.

This work—
the trying
    reframing
    gentleness
    rest
    uncovering
    sleep
    joy
    tending
    listening
    trusting
is VALID and NECESSARY to MOVE FORWARD.

This is the work.
This is living.

Words for the Pyre

Worthless.
Stupid.
Never going to amount to anything.
Waste of space.
Waste of time.
You'll just end up working at Wal-Mart.
Embarrassing.
Ignorant.
Disappointing.
Disgusting.
Don't eat that, you'll get fat.
Why wasn't it an A?
            - the words of my childhood

Worthless.
Everyone hates me.
Everyone is disappointed in me.
I'm not enough.
There's not enough time.
There's not enough me.
I can't do it all. I have to do it all.
I'll rest when I'm dead.
I'm responsible for their happiness.
If I don't do it, who will?
If I tiptoe around…I'll make it through.
Just stay quiet a little longer, next time I'll speak.
I'm a burden to everyone.
If I do everything, maybe that will shatter the cold shoulder.
If I over prepare they won't find me wanting.
Just one more thing, maybe then…

You'll never be accepted.

They're mad at you.

They're disappointed with you.

They wonder why you don't do more.

The more you serve, the more they'll know your love.

If you're not dying for others, are you even committed?

Keep your head down.

Hide your face. Hide your fat.

Keep a smile on your face.

Put on more make-up. Dress nice. Always presentable. That's the only way they won't point out your flaws.

Plan ahead. There can be no mistakes.

You've already failed.

You're behind.

You'll never catch up.

Why even try?

- the inner monologue of my 20s & 30s

From the Ashes

I am worthy, simply because I exist.
I carry dignity in my being as my inherent right endowed by
my Creator. It is neither given or taken.
I am not responsible for others' emotions.
I am not responsible for others' expectations.
I can rest right now.
I don't need to run myself ragged for love and acceptance.
I don't need to burn out for the sake of community, for the
love of God.
I am not the punching bag for others issues, be it anger or
insecurity.
Being fat is not a moral or spiritual failing.
My body is not my enemy.
My body is a part of me.
My body has carried me through grief after grief.
I am my body and my body is me. I am not a functioning
Gnostic.
My body and I are not for the perusal and opinion of others.
I have time. I have time. I have time.
I don't need to catch-up. I can begin where I am.
I can make mistakes.
I am safe.
I am whole.

How Do I Trust Myself?

How do I trust myself?
That ever present anxiety
roiling waves in the pit of my stomach
clenching my heart

who is squeezing and won't let go?
fear   fear   fear

how do I know I'm right?
how can I believe I have the answer,
when I've been told, trained, conditioned
to look anywhere but myself?

Trust is easy when you're a tree
falling into the arms
of the forest
         —but this stepping onto air?

Pep Talk to Myself

We're not here to measure up.
We're here to be our full selves,
bring who we already are,
and leave a trail of flourishing.

I am no longer here to measure up.
I am here to be my full self.
I am bringing who I already am
leaving a trail of flourishing.

Read Fairy Tales

"Read fairy tales," they said.
"You must,
at least for the children's sake."
What they didn't say,
What I didn't expect
was awakening within
the maiden, mother, crone
The wisdom of youth
The strength of the mother
The deep knowing of what is

"Read fairy tales," they said.
They didn't tell me
all the versions
of myself
I'd find.

For the children's sake.
      They said.

I read for my own.
Am I not also the child?

For the sake of the maiden,
For the sake of the mother,
For the sake of the crone,
      Read fairy tales.

A Request for Love

May you allow yourself to be loved today.
May you receive the love you are given today—
the gift of a friend, the hug of a child, the heartfelt declaration
of a lover.
May you refute the urge to push back and say, "No, not me.
Worthy of love is not true for me."
Call it what it is: a lie.
Allow yourself a brave moment,
an open heart and eyes to receive love.
In the end, only love remains. Even in all its complications.
There is nothing higher.
Love requires diligence and practice.
Self-examination to peel back the layers of pain.
Practice love.
Practice receiving.
Allow yourself to be loved today.

On Waking

I did not think
waking up would take
so long.
I imagined
it more like the dawn,
all at once.
But it is a garden
in early spring
with soggy fields
and tiny blades of
fluorescent life.

A Benediction

May uncertainty be met with curiosity instead of dread.
May anxiety be a reason to pause, breathe, and seek answers
rather than hide.
May depression be met with gentleness, not shame and
self-loathing.
May flowers breed joy and connect you to the earth.
May justice be found and truth lay heavy on the unjust.
May words heal and create, unbound.
May magic come to those who seek.
May uncertainty lead to new paths of greater knowing.
May love speak louder than shame.
May the pain of growth bloom to new possibilities.
> Go and be thyself, wildflower.
> Go and wake.

I thought there was a before. Before the waking.
But I've come to realize I was always waking up.

Acknowledgements

For a season of such intimate turmoil, there were few witnesses, but I'm grateful for those who were there.

Shelby, Rachel, Meghan, Kristen—who kept asking how I was doing when I pulled away from the world, listened to my frustrations and rants, or held space for my tears when I couldn't say anything.

Brandi—Your hand of friendship let me feel seen and be in a place I didn't need to be in charge. Thank you. Keep sending me all the sewing and gardening reels.

Andi, my counselor—we laugh often now, but those first months were—whew. I wouldn't be here without you. Thank you for being a safe space to bring all the parts of myself.

My Internet/Writer Friends—I wish these Instagram houses were closer. Thank you to Stephanie Ascough for making me think this was possible and for being a blossoming 40-something with me. To KJL for all the brave times you showed up and shared yourself. To so many—Beth, Kate, Emily, Marina and more—who show up and give yourself to this work. It matters. The doing, the witnessing, the showing up. It all matters.

To my CPs—Emily, Becky, and Nicole—who I maybe forgot to tell about this project until it was almost done. Oops. You invited me in when everything else was falling apart. Thanks for being a steady point and sharing stories.

To the WWTS community & the WWTS indie crew…we're doing this! I've been surprised by the near strangers who've come alongside, answered questions, and supported this work. Cheering you on! Send the pre-order link!

Thank you to writers and musicians (who will probably never read this) whose work was a lifeline in the dark and reminded me Light and Love were still waiting for me; particularly Seth Haines (*The Book of Waking Up*..how I cried working in my garden listening to this audiobook), K.J. Ramsey (*This Too Shall Last, The Lord is My Courage*), Roo Panes ("There Is a Place," "Land of the Living," "The Sun Will Rise Over the Year"), Emily Scott Robinson ("The Time for Flowers" and "Let 'Em Burn"), and Jess Ray ("Gallows," "Runaway").

My children—thank you for respecting the "writer at work" sign. You got it for me. I can only hope that you won't carry as much baggage as I. You're worthy of love, of hope, of belonging. I hope you are always waking to more wonder, freedom, and love.

Joe, my husband—What can I say? Thank you for being constant against my fears and lies. One day I'll believe you. Keep telling me the truth anyway. I'm still learning to receive it.

About the Author

Jess Lynn is a lover of stories, wearer of flower crowns, and still believes in magic. She writes for the girl who never grew up, for the one wondering if hope is a joke (she's been there too), and the one who sees wonder in the world.

She writes for people who aren't afraid to look for hope in strange places–haunted woods, myths, and family secrets. She finds inspiration in the truth that every thing, every person, every happenstance and history has its own story.

As one who lives between worlds and identities as a Native American (Lumbee Tribe of North Carolina), mother, and person of faith, she writes poetry and stories at the crossroads of history, fairy tales, and magic.

When her head's not stuck in a book or following rabbit trails of possible plot lines, she's busy building a life with her husband, mothering and homeschooling their four children, and ever so slowly renovating their 1917 farmhouse in South Carolina.

Also By

Poetry

The Wistful Wild: Fairy Tale Poems of Longing and Ferocity

an anthology with Stephanie Ascough (editor), Stephanie Escobar, Caitlin Gemmel, Courney Joseph, Beth Stedman

Links

Website

jesslynnbooks.com

Newsletter: *Between Worlds*

jesslynnbooks.com/newsletter

Instagram

www.instagram.com/jesslynnbooks

www.ingramcontent.com/pod-product-compliance
Lightning Source LLC
LaVergne TN
LVHW051423080426
835508LV00022B/3217